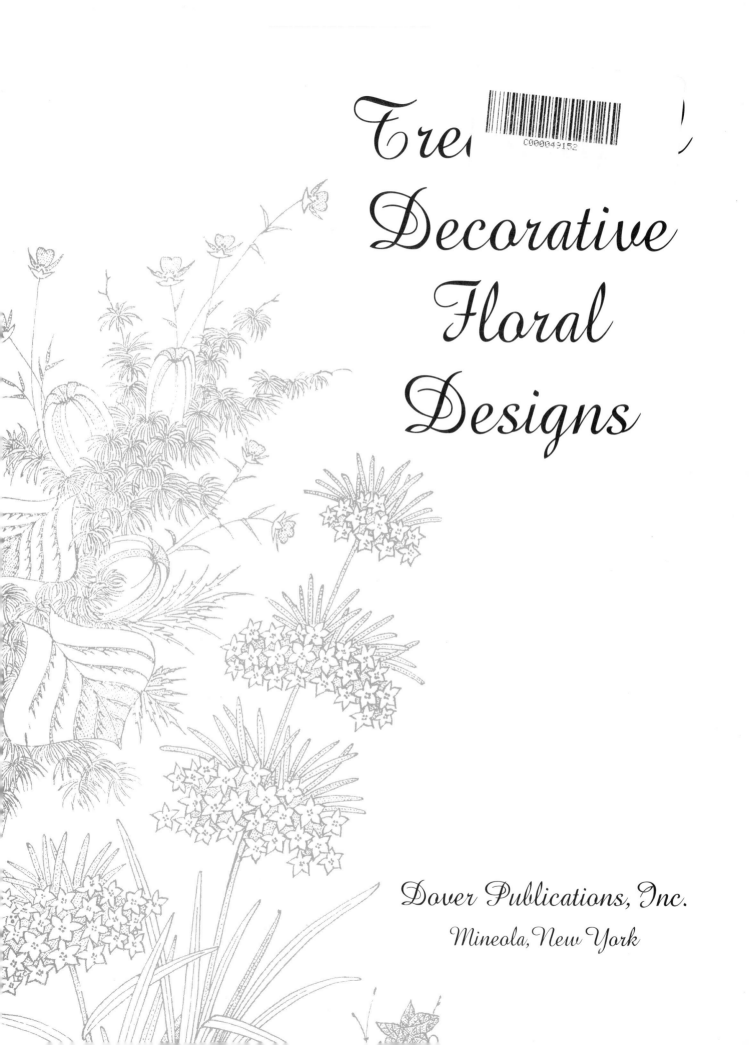

Tre... Decorative Floral Designs

Dover Publications, Inc.

Mineola, New York

Bibliographical Note

Treasury of Decorative Floral Designs is a new work, first published by Dover Publications, Inc., in 2005.

DOVER *Pictorial Archive* SERIES

Library of Congress Cataloging-in-Publication Data

Treasury of decorative floral designs / Dover.
 p. cm.—(Dover pictorial archive series)
 ISBN 0-486-44623-9 (pbk.)
 1. Decoration and ornament—Plant forms. I. Dover Publications, Inc. II. Series.

NK1560.T74 2005
743'.7—dc22

 2005047221

Manufactured in the United States of America
Dover Publications, Inc., 31 East 2nd Street, Mineola, N.Y. 11501

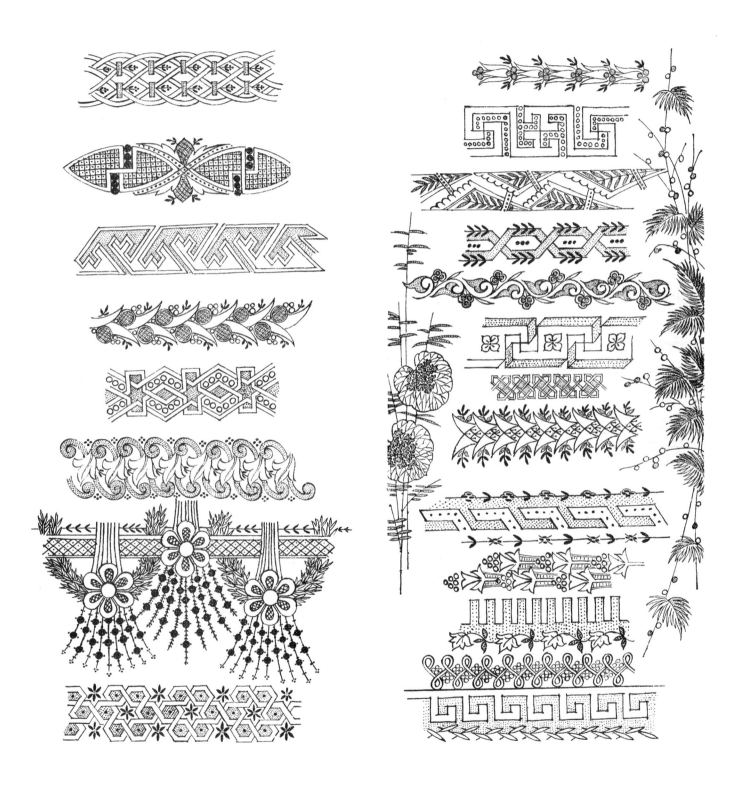

Plate 1

Plate 2

Plate 3

Plate 4

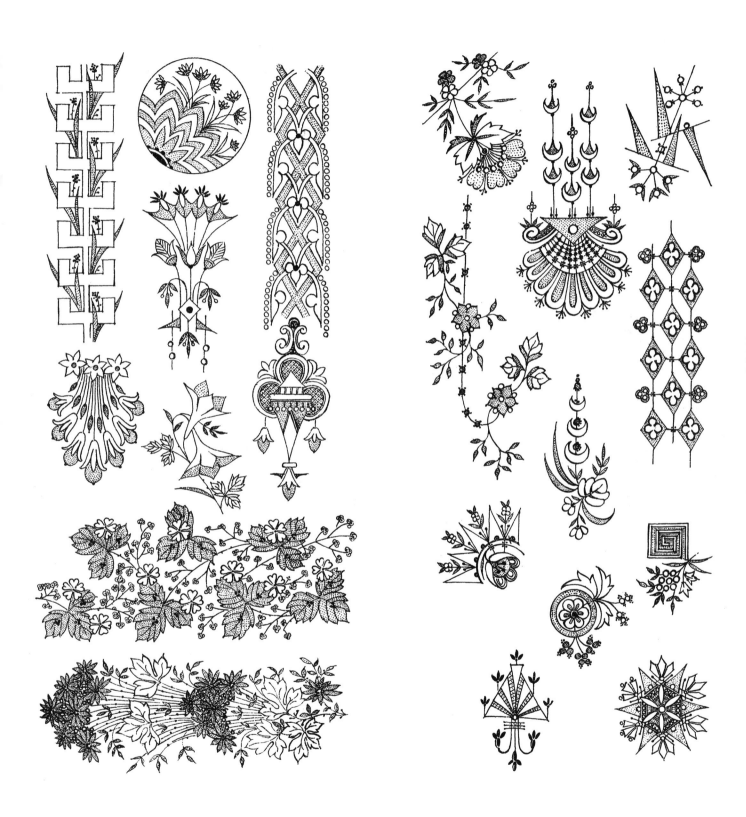

Plate 5

Plate 6

Plate 7

Plate 8

Plate 9

Plate 10

Plate 11

Plate 12

Plate 13

Plate 14

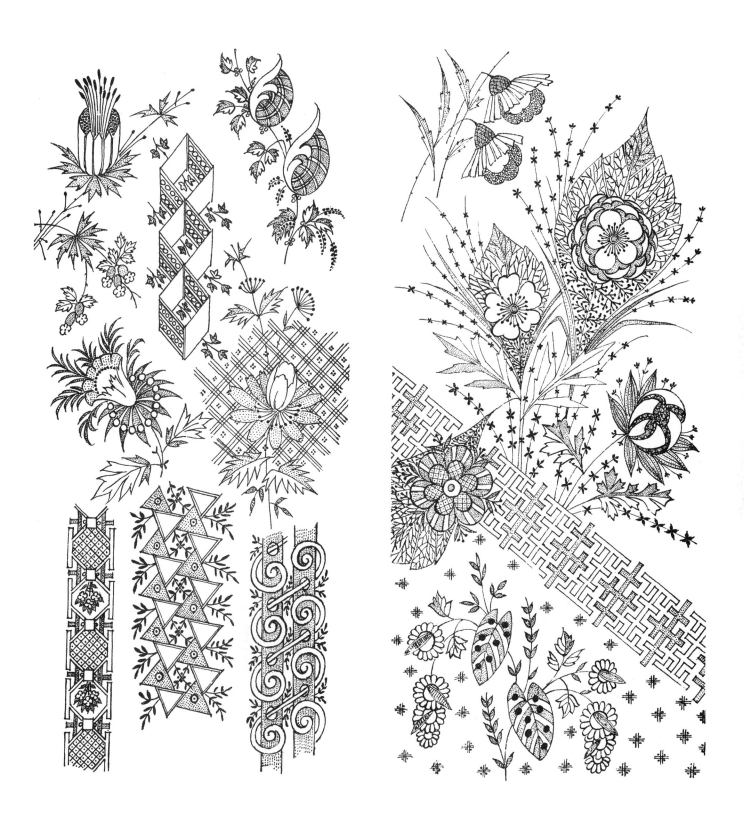

Plate 15

Plate 16

Plate 17

Plate 18

Plate 19

Plate 20

Plate 21

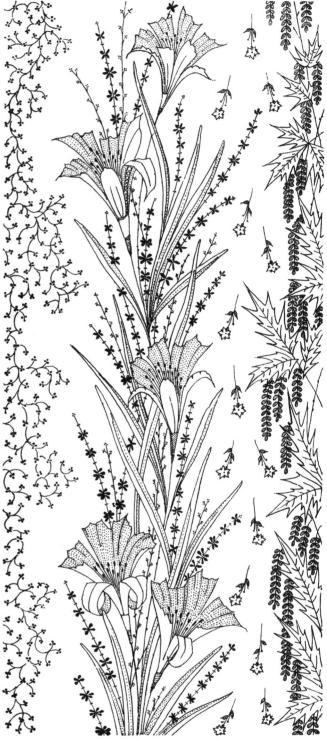

Plate 22

Plate 23

Plate 24

Plate 25

Plate 26

Plate 27

Plate 28

Plate 29

Plate 30

Plate 31

Plate 32

Plate 33

Plate 34

Plate 35

Plate 36

Plate 37

Plate 38

Plate 39

Plate 40

Plate 41

Plate 42

Plate 43

Plate 44

Plate 45

Plate 46